Mediumship Made Super Simple

Beginner Basics of Mediumship Development & Workbook

Aerin Kube, Ph.D

Copyright © 2021 Aerin Kube

All rights reserved. No part of this publication may be reproduced, distributed, or transmitted in any form or by any means, including photocopying, recording, or other electronic or mechanical methods, without the prior written permission of the publisher, except in the case of brief quotations embodied in critical reviews and certain other noncommercial uses permitted by copyright law.

This book may not be suitable for all ages. Any information provided is only shared from my education, opinion, and experience and not intended to take the place of any professional counselors, doctors, or clergy, etc.

The educational information provided within this book is for general informational purposes only. The author makes no representations or warranties, express or implied, about the completeness, accuracy, reliability, suitability, or availability concerning any information, products, or services in this book for any purpose. Any use of this information is at your own risk.

ISBN: 9798734704417

Library of Congress Control Number: 2021907351

Printed in the United States of America.

First printing edition 2021.

www.aerinkube.com

Dedication

To God, the angels, my husband, my children, and my family. This book is dedicated to you for your love and support.

Special thanks to my friends, teachers, and the spiritual community, especially Tina Panteli, my friend and assistant that spent countless hours supporting my work.

About the Author

Aerin is a Spiritual Author and Teacher. She earned a Ph.D. in Metaphysical Theology from the Univ. of Metaphysical Sciences, accredited by the American Alternative Medical Assoc.

As an Ordained Minister, she has trained under many renowned spiritual leaders and is a professional and certified psychic medium and remote viewer.

Before the unfoldment of her spiritual journey, she worked in corporate America. Having attended secular colleges and universities, she received degrees in business and human science.

Her knowledge and strengths come from her experience in teaching, writing, counseling, real estate, marketing, theater, and public speaking, as well as her past as a successful entrepreneur of a renowned multi-location operation for expectant families around Michigan.

Aerin holds certifications in Reiki, IET, life coaching, and mediumship. Her passion is psychical studies, parapsychology, philosophy, and helping others see the light within them.

AerinKube.com

Table of Contents

CHAPTER 1: WHAT IS A MEDIUM? 3

CHAPTER 2: CAN ANYONE BECOME A MEDIUM? 5

CHAPTER 3: WHY DO YOU WANT TO BECOME A MEDIUM? 7

CHAPTER 4: ARE YOU WILLING AND READY TO COMMIT? 11

CHAPTER 5: HOW DO I KNOW IF I AM A MEDIUM? 13

CHAPTER 6: SHOULD I BE FEARFUL OF MEDIUMSHIP? 17

CHAPTER 7: HOW DOES INFORMATION COME THROUGH TO ME? 23

CHAPTER 8: WHAT ARE MY STRONGEST CLAIRS? 27

CHAPTER 9: WHAT ARE THE DIFFERENT TYPES OF MEDIUMSHP? 37

CHAPTER 10: WHAT SHOULD I DO TO PREPARE? 39

CHAPTER 11: WHAT ARE SPIRIT GUIDES AND HOW CAN THEY HELP? 43

CHAPTER 12: WHAT IS SITTING IN THE POWER? 47

CHAPTER 13: CAN YOU TELL ME HOW TO CONNECT? 51

CHAPTER 14: WHAT ARE SOME ADDITIONAL THINGS TO CONSIDER? 57

CHAPTER 15 FINAL WORDS 71

Greetings

If you are reading this book, you are most likely looking to become a psychic medium. Perhaps you already know you are a medium and seek helpful ways to increase your links with Spirit. Maybe you have lost a loved one and swear you can feel their energy around you. Just having reassurance can undoubtedly help the grieving process for many people.

You may or may not have learned that we are all psychic intuitive souls. We can further develop our spiritual awareness where we can connect with higher dimensions.

If you have questions about the simple basics of beginning mediumship, this book will hopefully help you uncover some truths. It will give you a jump start to learn about the Spirit World.

It is here that I can help you with tips, ideas, and thoughts, but it's you that will make it happen. Each one of us must find the faith, trust, and knowledge that we have this incredible ability already within us. Understanding this concept may be more difficult for some people.

Our souls are bright and beautiful rays of sunshine that can get clouded by the doubts, fears, and worries of society and a lifetime of experiences. These memories may have left less than perfect imprints on us. There could have been events in life that might have affected a person's journey making it feel tougher. It's up to us as we move along our spiritual path to learn how to release those old footprints. By doing so, we can raise our vibration higher, to feel lighter and brighter with more trust and faith than we have ever known.

Welcome To The World Of Psychic Mediumship

Welcome to the start of your new spiritual journey towards understanding your soul and the Spirit World better. I'm so glad you are here and that I can help you get started.

This book aims to be short and easy to read. It is only to provide you with some simple and basic information. Realize that there is a wealth of knowledge out there to learn when you are ready to progress.

So many teachers have written excellent books that will further your development. When looking for new information to help you grow, consider exploring what you feel pulled to read. Sometimes we don't always discover everything we need in one place. It's best to find your answers and truths along your journey. Everything will come in the time it should, and when it does, it will make sense and feel right.

One thing I can tell you that is most important is to keep an open mind so that you are never judging another's journey or beliefs. Being a medium and a teacher, I have found this is common in the spiritual community. We are all having a human experience and developing at different stages. Our backgrounds, experiences, and abilities, for instance, all are unique to us. It would help if you didn't ever believe that your viewpoints on metaphysics are more accurate than others. You don't want your ego ever to be a problem in your development.

No matter how far advanced you become, when moving forward, always remember my words about remaining open-minded. We can't judge the experiences of others as being right or wrong. Instead, focus on what makes you unique and how you can help yourself, your soul, and those you encounter.

Increasing spiritual awareness is a process and not meant to get rushed. While we are developing, we are raising our vibration. In doing so, we release and heal what doesn't serve us.

Always remember the journey forward is yours, and it must be true to you. It doesn't matter what other people think or feel about your path and beliefs. They don't walk in your shoes and have not experienced your soul's journey thus far.

If you can remember that and are ready to begin trusting yourself and the Spirit World, you are prepared for this beautiful trek forward. Let's get started.

Chapter 1
What Is A Medium?

Are you ready? Of course, you are, and I'm thrilled for you! You wish to become a medium, someone that can communicate with the deceased and bridge the gap between those living and those in Spirit. Each class I've held with new faces preparing to become mediums, I'm always excited, hopeful, and confident. I wish all students to find the door that will bring greater awareness of what is beyond the physical. That way, the dream of becoming a medium turns into a reality in time.

We all have the God-given gift of psychic intuition. Being psychic is different than being a medium. However, understanding and accepting your psychic ability and senses is essential to the process's first step. You see, mediums take their developing psychic intuition a step further to connect with those crossed over.

Reading on a psychic level is not the same as the link you hold during mediumship, but it is similar in that the information communicated comes through your same psychic senses or clairs. We will go over these in a later chapter.

When it comes to psychic mediumship abilities, most of us don't understand or acknowledge our gift and power. We may or may not know that it is there and that we can learn to tap into it to explore beyond our ordinary senses. That is until we have an experience that makes us question if we are not alone. Sometimes, we see, hear, or feel things that we don't understand and desire to find answers to recognize and communicate with Spirit. On the other hand, some people have experienced it throughout their lives and wish to develop finally.

Working with new students, I've found they all come in with different emotions, expectations, and experiences. Often, people are excited and can't wait to get started. They want to link with Spirit to communicate with their loved ones crossed over. While there are students who already know they can communicate, they wish to understand better how to link and hold it.

Still, some come in with a desire to understand what is suddenly going on around them. Many students may hold fear from a lifetime of society's judgments and beliefs, but they wish to discover the positive to begin to embrace their new ability.

No matter your circumstance, realize that the power is within you to get started on learning mediumship and enhancing your spiritual awareness to recognize the signs of the Spirit World.

Chapter 2
Can Anyone Become A Medium?

There are differing messages spread across the internet, in classes, books, and discussions about whether one must be born naturally as a medium. Some people swear that you cannot become a medium, while others believe you can choose to learn how to be a medium. I don't have all the answers, and you can formulate in time what your belief is on this subject.

Based on what I have witnessed, my personal feeling is that anyone can learn to become a medium. I don't think it's a special ability granted only to specific individuals. Though, I believe that some people are more naturally gifted and find it easier to learn. They may develop their mediumship to a very heightened level that others may not reach.

Some folks have worked on their skills for years and still struggle with their links, but they have had one or more rich experiences that they usually can share. At the very least, they have learned how to identify Spirit to know when they are around and how to receive signs. They may not always understand or feel they have a strong enough link to obtain more profound messages, but they do pick up evidence, even if very minute.

Nevertheless, they have within them the ability to work and hone the gift, thus making me believe that we can all possess the power in some way. The more time you spend developing, the better you get. It's like that with anything in life, so try and remember that. If you wish to be good at something, you must believe in yourself and trust that at the right time, everything will get accomplished.

Like any skill, there will always be those individuals who seem to master an ability. They may be able to do it fast and not understand why or how. It comes naturally, and if you were to ask them how they did it, often they couldn't tell you. It just happened, like how some people pick up a paintbrush one day and create a masterpiece.

No matter which person you are or how fast, easy, or hard developing mediumship may be, always remember something important. Mediumship is not a race or competition, and there is no finish line. We are forever students learning to hone our ability. When working on your mediumship, have patience, trust, don't judge yourself or others, or compare yourself. Mediumship is not about you! True mediumship is about the connection with Spirit to bring incredible love and healing through. Whether it is for yourself or others, it should always get viewed as a God-given gift.

Chapter 3
Why Do You Want To Become A Medium?

Have you asked yourself why you wish to explore and develop yourself as a medium? I bring this to your attention because I think it's a good question that I frequently ask students at the very beginning. People will often tell me it's because of the healing and love that come through it. They desire to be of service and to help spread light to those around them. I believe mediumship has come a long way in the last few decades. It has risen to new heights, and its effects are now getting seen by society as a healing modality.

If you were to look back at the history of mediumship, you would see the positive changes that have slowly developed over time. For many years, mediums got looked upon as negative and fraudulent. Some in society still feel this way and are skeptical; however, many people see the truth and value of good mediumship.

If you ever would like to explore the history of mediumship, consider researching and reading up on Spiritualism. It has a long history that dates back. Though it's not something I intend to cover in this book because it's a religion, it is fascinating and encompasses a lot of material. It may help you understand the foundation of mediumship, especially if you should seek to become a Spiritualist. Even if you choose not to adopt the religion, I think it is still important as a developing medium to recognize its historical significance.

Over the last few decades, great pioneers of mediumship helped open many eyes worldwide. Because of these people, we can now walk and talk freely about our ability. We do not feel as judged as those in the past.

Television shows nowadays focusing on the supernatural engross large audiences around the world. More people than ever are opening and wishing to explore the paranormal. Many mediums are now looked up to and sought out for teaching or readings for healing, guidance, and more.

Most people fail to recognize the effort these terrific mediums have put into their work and how much they learned along the way. Even those who would consider themselves natural still put in a lot of time and energy. For many TV or well-known long-time mediums, they sacrificed a great deal to bring mediumship into the forefront where healing and proof of the afterlife exists.

As you are stepping into this new area, take a moment and ask yourself some questions. For instance, are you desiring to make a difference in the world and help bring people upward to a place where healing can happen? Do you want to experience mediumship for yourself to help with grief? Do you know you have the ability or feel you have it and wish to explore and develop to be the voice of Spirit for others? Do you want to prove that life goes on even after the body's physical death? If you answered yes to anything that will help yourself and provide comfort, love, and healing for others, then you are on the right path.

Why Do You Wish To Become A Medium?

_____

_____

_____

_____

_____

_____

_____

_____

_____

_____

_____

_____

_____

Chapter 4
Are You Willing and Ready To Commit?

Are you ready to honestly invest time in your development? I hope so, as I have seen numerous people stop working at their mediumship because they can't commit or lose interest. As you read this book, I praise you for taking the time and making an effort. It's a start to the journey forward that you will need a lot of patience, especially early on.

You may have heard the sayings or understand that there is a reason when something is well worth waiting for. Nothing happens overnight, everything happens in the time it should, and dedication is vital. When it comes to developing your mediumship, you are also working to elevate, enlighten and heal your soul. Time spent learning and practicing with Spirit will bring you copious amounts of love and excitement mixed with moments of frustration.

It's your job to understand that not everything will be easy, and there will be times you may wish to quit. Of course, you may have to do so on the journey if life requires you to shift your focus for a while. Remember, though, that it's not a race and your ability to take care of yourself and your family comes first.

When you do decide to focus on your mediumship, do not try and find shortcuts. Committing to Spirit to do the work for the right reasons means that you must travel the path to learn the most you can. A good medium will develop slowly and with the proper dedication. Remember that your job is to help others and be an authentic voice for the Spirit World. Shortcutting the process can make it more difficult to sustain good solid links for communication. Also, when you find the path to healing, you can better communicate. I believe Spirit often comes through with messages that attempt to heal their loved ones.

Make a mental note or even write your goals down on a piece of paper or in a journal where you can see them every day. Work with Spirit is the most enjoyable job on the planet, but it can also be challenging and cause a lot of heartache to those you may meet if you should skirt the process and not put in the right amount of time in understanding. Right now, make a commitment that you will do all that you can to help yourself and others on the journey toward bringing more love and light into the world.

Chapter 5
How Do I Know
If I Am A Medium?

If you read through chapter two, you might already have an idea of what I will say. However, let's recall and identify what you know already from your past experiences. Ask yourself why you wanted to buy and read this book. If you were curious, take time to meditate on why that might be. Perhaps you have noticed a strange phenomenon or have had vivid dreams with deceased loved ones or faces you didn't recognize. Have you considered your dreams to be the Spirit's way of visiting you? It's common and due in part to the fact that our mind is at rest, in a different state, and considered free from external noise during the waking hours. Generally, it happens to many people when they are beginning to fall asleep and upon waking.

Do you understand your psychic ability and your clairs? Have you done any research on psychic development yet? If you don't already know for sure about your clairs or the psychic senses, then we can cover that next. I have another book out that is called *Psychic Made Super Simple.* It's a short read that details basics and holds exercises and tips to support your development and strengthen psychic intuition. To help understand a few simple fundamentals you need for mediumship, I have included some of what is in that book here in case you haven't yet learned about basic psychic development. There are certain things you will need to know.

Right now, let's focus first on what signs you may have noticed in the past or are currently experiencing. Often, people have this idea that mediums see and hear Spirit like they do in the movies and on television. At one time, I thought that to be a true medium; you should see them like they were still living. I had no idea that mediumship was mostly telepathy and that the signs and messages of Spirit could be subtle.

Ask yourself if you can remember a time when you felt heavy, cold, or hot energy in a room with you or believed you were getting watched. Have you ever seen anything from the corner of your eyesight, like shadows, orbs, lights, or something fly by you that you couldn't be sure of what it was?

How about your hearing, taste, or smell of something or someone not present? Have you ever experienced a perfume or smell that you recognized as one related to someone crossed over? Possibly you thought of them at that moment as well. Perhaps you heard a departed loved ones' words drift in at just the right moment, giving you the advice you needed, or you tasted the flavor of one of grandma's recipes from out of the blue.

Maybe you sat down on your couch one day to put on the television or the radio and abruptly thought about your loved one. You could even potentially see them in your mind, and they appear for a split second as vivid to you as if they were alive. These are all possible signs of Spirit, but many times, it may just be as simple as a coin on the floor, feather, or bird outside. You might think of your loved one and then see numbers on a sign that are synchronistic, like 444 or 222.

There might have been a moment that you thought of a loved one and then walked out to your car to see a butterfly sitting on the roof. Instantly, you question if it was a sign.

There are a variety of ways that Spirit can and will approach us. Developing yourself is the best way to find out. As I said in the earlier chapter, I believe that we could all learn to hone and harness the ability to some degree. Why not allow yourself the opportunity to explore it and find out.

Can You Recall Or Recognize Spiritual Energy That Was Present At Some Point That You Felt?

Chapter 6
Should I Be Fearful Of Mediumship?

Fear was a difficult subject at the beginning of my journey, especially during my awakening. I understand now that I had to work through my fears to be more empowered over my abilities. Learning and working with the Spirit World, you realize the amazing grace and love surrounding us every day, providing guidance and protection.

I want to mention that some of you may be thinking, *I'm not fearful. I'm ready and can't wait to connect with Spirit.* Yes, I know students who come in so excited to learn without fear holding them back, and I always admire and appreciate that. In my opinion, they seem to have an easier time because they don't have to release any worry or doubt regarding the Spirit World, thus allowing them to focus on their abilities.

Looking back, I know my scary moments were brought on through various reasons, like past, society, upbringing, religion, etc. When I first started, I came across a few people that were psychics and mediums. I turned to them, looking for advice and assistance with my gifts. Several of them were helpful, while others were not, especially since I was beginning my journey and felt frightened. Looking back, I can see that a few of them were still holding onto many fears themselves. When they tried to guide me, they inadvertently passed on more fear-based beliefs. It created an abundance of anxiety and worry that I know now was made worse by giving it attention and power.

Since we all have our belief systems and experiences, I will not dive deep into the world of metaphysics to prove or deny the existence of anything. Instead, I keep an open mind. What I will share, however, is that what we focus our energy on is what we will get in return. If you haven't heard of the saying or understand that *like attracts like,* you need to know that it is real. Also, the power of the mind is incredible, just as the power you hold within you. Understand that having faith is essential if you wish to move beyond fear to a place where only love exists.

Someone quoted the Bible once early on and then asked me if I had the faith of the mustard seed. Because I didn't, I couldn't answer or understand how that could help me. Over time, I realized what that truly meant, and I evolved to a place where there was no doubt. My relationship with God is more profound than I could have ever imagined since working with the Spirit World and seeing the love and healing that comes through every day.

If you ask me now, fear should never get tied into being psychic or a medium. The problem we have had over time is that people have labeled psychics and mediums as bad. The terms made people feel uncomfortable and still do for some in society.

For many developing mediums or those discovering their abilities, fear could force them to stop moving forward. You do not want to have doubts or worry over your natural gifts and the Spirit World. You must learn how to trust. For some of us, that is difficult but an obstacle that must get overcome.

As you develop, you will realize that you are always protected, loved, and supported by the Divine and that nothing evil can harm you when you are seeking love, healing, and guidance. No one can take away your power unless you give it to them. Remember that so you don't allow yourself to think otherwise.

In this next section, I will go over the causes of fear to help those of you that this may still be a concern. If it's not an issue, then you may wish to skip to the next chapter.

Fear of Being Wrong
Some people working as mediums fear they will bring in the wrong information and get looked at negatively. You must know that you will have good days and not so good days. Accept you are human and are not perfect. Those that continuously strive for perfection are working from their ego. Always do the best you can, being honest, sincere, and trusting of what you receive.

Religious Perspectives
Some religions believe that those who consult with psychics and mediums are evil because they receive from a dark source. We know today that is not the truth and more of an ancient perspective. People of faith are starting to realize this and questioning the earlier beliefs. There was a time where man created some aspects of certain religions to place control over society. One thing to consider if you are concerned with this is that in many religions, like Jesus and Mohammed, there was prophecy and spiritual healing phenomena.

Fear of The Unknown
Some people still place a superstitious perspective upon it. They continue to view it as bad, primarily due to no real rational or scientific answers. Not everything is going to have an explanation, and that scares people. We must come to our realizations and truths on our journey.

Charlatans and Frauds
Some individuals are practicing mediums and psychics that steal money from others with poor intentions. These people take away the legitimacy of what we do and make us look bad, giving the reputation of fraud. Do your best to release these people and remind yourself of your intentions to do good with your mediumship. Break free from what you cannot control and let

go of what others think. Remind yourself of your loving authenticity and positive objective.

Afraid of What Others Will Think

Many people are scared to come out of the "closet" in fear of what others will say. They worry people won't agree, especially in families and friendships where the others hold fearful views on psychics and mediums. They are afraid they might be looked at funny or called crazy or evil. Understand that you can't control how they think, only how you react. It's your life's path to find what makes you happiest. Not everyone will always agree with your decisions, but you must know that you are ultimately in charge. If you believe that it's best to do the work quietly, then that is your choice. You don't have to go around and tell everyone until you are ready to. For some people, that may take years or never happen. Just don't feel guilty or blame yourself for having the ability.

Are You Afraid Of Mediumship? Why or Why Not?

Can You Think Of Any Positive Affirmations Or Actions You Can Make To Accept Mediumship?

Chapter 7
How Does Information Come Through To Me?

About now, you may be wondering how, why, or where the information comes from that we receive. Perhaps you already know, but I will go over it quickly. Everything in the universe, including us, is made up of energy. We can learn to read this energy because it is everywhere and in motion. Understand that our loved ones crossed over are also energy because only the physical body dies. The energy of the soul lives on, and we connect and link to that during communication.

 We can use our sixth sense, or the clairs, to receive information by allowing images, impressions, and feelings to come in. When our mind is quiet and relaxed, then we can tap in and read that energy easier. Consider it a gift from the universe or your Creator, God, or a Divine Source depending on your beliefs.

 If you have never considered any of this before, it may seem like a lot to take in, but we are all capable of reading energy in some form or another, and we do it almost daily without thinking about it. Everyone can feel energy. Go back and recall a time when you walked into a crowded area. How did the room feel to you? Was it positive or negative? Did it cause any anxiety or excitement? If yes, realize you were experiencing the feel of the energy emitted.

When you stand next to someone in a bad or good mood, can you feel it? Though you might not understand how you receive, you feel it through the psychic clair called clairsentience. That specific sense is one of the most used and can provide so much information about the world around us. People don't generally look at it that way or understand it completely.

Maybe this is an excellent time to talk about the clairs. Besides our ordinary physical senses, everyone has within them psychic senses. It's also known as a sixth sense. There was once a time that I believed that only special people had a sixth sense. I learned otherwise. When God, a Higher Power, created us, He gave us natural intuition to survive. We often call this instinct. Our physical senses of seeing, hearing, feeling, tasting, and smelling are familiar to us. When it comes to our sixth sense, we have those same intuits but in a non-physical way. We can experience them from within us, and they are called clairs.

Clairvoyance – Clear Seeing

Clairaudience – Clear Hearing

Clairsentience – Clear Feeling

Claircognizance – Clear Knowing

Clairgustance – Clear Tasting

Clairalience – Clear Smelling

All of the clairs can be present in everyone. From my experience, often one or two of them is stronger and tends to bring in more reliable information from the Divine, Spirit World, and the energy around us, etc. These clairs can help you receive both psychically and mediumistically and provide you with messages, images, sounds, feelings, and impressions depending on the type of link and your intention.

We can learn to develop and strengthen the clairs to better communicate faster with greater understanding and clarity. If you wish to build them, practice is vital. You can find some great exercises online and through other metaphysical books that offer tips, activities, and more.

Before I end this chapter, I believe it might be beneficial to include the "Clairs Quiz" that I provided in my other book, *Psychic Made Super Simple*, which holds exercises for developing the clairs. I think the quiz will help you to identify which of the above clairs get most used. It does help when you are receiving, in my opinion. If you have already read the other book or know your strongest senses, then perhaps taking the quiz might only help to see if your abilities have progressed and strengthened to include new clairs that weren't first recognized. It's up to you if you should decide to skip the quiz.

One thing I will add is that our senses as we develop will change and progress. It's best to learn to grow and utilize as many clairs as you can from my experience. Practice, patience, and time will help to get them to work in harmony.

I mention this because clairvoyance might bring in a vision of someone, while clairaudience tells you who it is, and clairsentience allows you to know more about them and their personality. That is just an example that I provided. No one clair is better than another, but it can act as a better receiver for you if it's stronger from my perspective. Go ahead and take the quiz to see what clairs might be your strongest right now.

Chapter 8
What Are My Strongest Clairs

"Which clairs do I have?" That is one of the first questions often asked when people have identified that they are psychic. Students wish to know what to develop and how to grow. I have created a short little list of questions for my classes and two different ways to help find the answer.

Part I. Clairs Test
Ask yourself from the list below which statements you can identify. Put a checkmark on each that applies to you.

Clairvoyance

- ☐ I have a detailed and vivid recollection of things that happen.

- ☐ I sometimes see flashes of light, shadows, orbs, and images.

☐ I love looking at art, photographs, or going to museums.

☐ I daydream or dream vividly at night.

☐ I can easily see pictures and images with my eyes closed or open.

Clairaudience

☐ I love music and often hear it in my head.

☐ I love listening to a great story, and I always lend an ear to a friend.

☐ I enjoy listening to the sounds of nature.

☐ I like to listen to the radio or podcasts.

☐ Sometimes I hear my name getting called, and no one is present.

Claircognizance

☐ I know things sometimes instantly.

☐ I get lots of inspiration from out of the blue.

☐ I am always thinking of new ideas and enjoy writing.

☐ I sometimes know what others are thinking.

Clairsentience

☐ I don't usually like crowded places as I feel strange.

☐ I sometimes know when others aren't feeling well physically or emotionally.

☐ I can feel when others are in pain on a physical level.

- ☐ I can walk in somewhere and feel the energy.
- ☐ Sometimes I can touch something and feel a vibration.

Clairalience

- ☐ I can sometimes smell perfume when none is around.
- ☐ I can sometimes smell food before it gets cooked.
- ☐ I can smell what someone is eating from over the telephone or at a distance.
- ☐ When hearing a story, I can sometimes smell something relating to the story.

Clairgustance

- ☐ I can sometimes taste the food that others have eaten.
- ☐ I sometimes get strange tastes in my mouth. i.e., smoke, tar, coal, etc.
- ☐ Sometimes I walk through the store and can taste something on a shelf without eating it.
- ☐ I can think of food and can taste a little of the flavor in my mouth.

Now that you have completed the list, can you identify which clair(s) you checked off the most statements? Let's try another exercise that looks at strength.

CLAIRS STRENGTH TEST

Clairvoyance – The Seeing Clair
When you are seeing, it's said to be with your third eye. This eye is right between the brows and works in connection with your pineal gland. Think of seeing with your third eye to visualize and paint an image easily inside your mind.

Exercise 1: Clairvoyance

To begin, you will close your eyes and take a couple of deep breaths doing your best to visualize white light around your body, encapsulating it.

Was that successful? _____

Next, try and think of someone you talked to recently and close your eyes and see if you can visualize them. Take notice if you can see what they are wearing. Can you see any colors or anything significant in detail?

Was that successful? _____

Exercise 2: Clairvoyance
On a scale of 1 -5, on an average day, how easy is seeing in your mind, receiving visions, or daydreaming?

1. Impossible
2. Rare
3. Sometimes
4. Often
5. Always

Clairaudience – The Hearing Clair

This clair is hearing, but it's not with your ears exactly. Most of this sense can be heard from inside your head. You may be able to hold conversations in your mind. For instance, it could be a voice that gives you an answer back inside your head after questioning something.

Exercise 1: Clairaudience

1. Yes or No – Do you talk inside your head?

2. Yes or No – Do you hear an answer-back?

3. Yes or No - Does that voice say "You" rather than "I"?

4. Yes or No - Do you ever quickly hear a word or name in your head?

5. Yes or No – Does music get stuck or play in your head?

Exercise 2: Clairaudience

On a scale of 1 -5, how often do you hear thoughts or phrases or music in your head?

1. Never
2. Rare
3. Sometimes
4. Often
5. Always

Clairsentience – The Feeling Clair

I bet you can recognize this one, and you use it almost every day to some varying degree, depending on how sensitive you are. This clair is one of feeling. Many people that consider themselves empaths will relate. You might feel it emotionally, mentally, or physically.

Exercise 1: Clairsentience

1. Yes or No - Can you feel the energy when you walk into a room?

2. Yes or No - Can you sense if the energy is good or bad feeling?

3. Yes or No - Do you notice when someone is upset before they say it?

4. Yes or No - Do you ever feel great and then suddenly feel different after you have been around someone angry, tired, or sad?

Exercise 2: Clairsentience
On a scale of 1 -5, based on the questions above, how often does this happen, or do you notice it?

1. Never
2. Rare
3. Sometimes
4. Often
5. Always

Clairgustance – The Tasting Clair
This clair is tasting food or non-food items when you have not put it in your mouth.

Exercise 1: Clairgustance

1. Yes or No - Have you ever gotten a taste of something that you didn't eat?

2. Yes or No – Have you ever tasted a food just thinking about it?

Exercise 2: Clairgustance
On a scale of 1- 5, how often would you say that you experience tasting?

1. Never experienced
2. Rare
3. Sometimes
4. Often
5. Very

Clairalience – The Smelling Clair
This clair is smelling scents that are not present.

Exercise 1: Clairalience

1. Yes or No – Have you ever smelled perfume or smoke in a room where there was no perfume or smoke?

2. Yes or No – Have you ever smelled anything strange and questioned where it was coming from only to find no reason?

Exercise 2: Clairalience
On a scale of 1- 5, how often would you say that you experience these smells?

1. Never experienced
2. Rare
3. Sometimes
4. Often
5. Very

Claircognizance – The Knowing Clair
This clair can be harder to detect. You may receive creative or inspiring ideas. You may also just know things at times instantly and not know why. It's like magical knowledge that just pops in.

Exercise 1: Claircognizance

1. Yes or No – I always seem to know what to say to help people feel better.

2. Yes, or No – Words always flow out of my mouth, and I can write just the same.

3. Yes or No – Sometimes, I talk to my pets, and I know what they are thinking back to me.

Exercise 2: Claircognizance

On a scale of 1- 5, how often does it happen where you just know stuff but can't explain how.

1. Never
2. Rare
3. Sometimes
4. Often
5. Always

Now that you finished these exercises, go back over them to see what stands out for you. Can you see which clairs you identified with easily? Can you see through completing exercise #2 which clair is most often used and strongest? Were you surprised?

Your stronger senses can help you receive and get guidance from the Divine. As you begin to practice and develop these senses, you will need to learn to trust the information. If you have other clairs identified but not as strong, know that you can grow them. In time, you can utilize the clairs and get them to work in harmony together. It will take time and practice, so be patient with yourself.

EXERCISE: JOURNAL YOUR DEVELOPING CLAIRS

Part I. My strongest psychic clairs are:
Write down which clairs you felt are strongest based on the results or your belief.

_____

_____

_____

_____

Part II. My experiences with using my psychic clairs.
Sit quietly and recall when you may have experienced using your clairs and didn't realize it. Look back in six months and review this information to see your progress.

_____

_____

_____

_____

_____

Chapter 9
What Are The Different Types of Mediumship?

There are different types of mediumship, but I will only identify which ones are more widely known. I do not wish to make it complicated in a beginner's book. There is a lot of information out there to research if you would like different views, perspectives, and greater detail. In this book, we will focus on Mental Mediumship because it is the most common.

Mental Mediumship
This form of mediumship is where a medium communicates with Spirit using telepathy through consciousness. The medium blends with Spirit to receive evidential information through the clairs to show proof of the afterlife. Spirit impresses into the medium's mind and body, thoughts, feelings, and images.

Trance Mediumship
This form is a type of mental mediumship. Generally, in most cases, the medium remains conscious during communication with the Spirit. In this form of mediumship, Spirit will use the medium's mind to impress thoughts, feelings, words, etc., to

influence and convey messages. There are deeper trance states where the medium may not remember or be aware of all messages they verbalized through their body and voice. It happens in a self-induced hypnotic trance.

Physical Mediumship

This form of mediumship is where Spirit can physically manifest and manipulate by use of the medium. The medium may take on mannerisms and actions of the deceased. People in the room attending, sometimes called a séance, can physically hear, feel, or see the phenomena occurring in front of them. Examples of this type include automatic writing, direct voice, materialization, transfiguration, white noise, levitation, apport, or physical material during the session. If you wish for more information, research physical mediumship, and learn about this incredibly rare ability.

The above three are listed here to make it easier for you as a beginner. Based on my experience, there are a lot of misconceptions and differing viewpoints. Many mediums, it seems, can combine trance with mental mediumship and physical with trance. It may seem confusing to the new learner, especially at first.

If you ask my opinion, it is not essential when starting. Your journey will unfold in time, and Spirit will take you where you are needed. You may find that your abilities carry you further than you imagined. No matter what type of medium you are or become, understand that all mediumship requires you to develop power and knowledge over time. The best mediums heal themselves and work extensively on training and practicing. They know that the medium's role is to share healing, love, guidance, and most importantly, prove human existence after death, demonstrating that life is eternal.

Chapter 10
What Should I Do To Prepare Me?

We will now focus on meditation and why your spiritual journey needs to unfold. You might have heard already that regular meditation can help overall well-being. For some people, the idea of beginning meditation creates anxiety. I hear all the time from students that it is not easy.

It is more difficult from my own experience at the beginning and sometimes when you are incredibly stressed. However, you can learn to do it, and it's beneficial, especially if you are feeling tension, anxiety, and overwhelm. Meditation is known to help create balance, increase confidence, stamina, energy, inner peace, and much more.

Besides creating a healthier you, you also expand your spiritual awareness by doing meditation, thereby increasing your psychic mediumship abilities.

You must find the time to set aside consistently. Even a few minutes daily to sit in your energy will help calm the mind from the outside world's noise. Everyday pressures surround us, and this causes our minds to become filled with thoughts and sounds of mindless chatter. It gets said that we often think way too much. Meditation can help us alleviate and quiet the commotion in our head to go within to a peaceful and trancelike state that will help us receive from Spirit.

So now, let's focus on starting the meditation process if you haven't already begun or found something that works for you. If you are one of those concerned with not having time to meditate or can't seem to fit it into your schedule, try it for short periods. Don't make it much longer than five minutes if that is the case. Try meditation little by little to learn to develop it. It's no different than setting aside time to go to the gym. You may not be able to last long during those first couple of gym visits, but as you know, you will get stronger and better at it the more you do it. You may soon find that it will become a habit.

I express to people starting meditation they don't need to put stringent rules on how or when they meditate. Some people do it daily and for hours, while others do it when they can. In my opinion, it doesn't matter how or where you meditate, so long as you find a way to give yourself time. Strive daily or at least a few times a week. If a schedule is best for you or you desire to further your skills in meditation, seek out books. There are many out there to help with this.

Once meditation becomes a regular part of your day, you may find it helpful to have a specific time and space set aside. Some people swear it helps to have a dedicated sacred space for meditation. I agree and often tell students to make a regular appointment with Spirit if they can. In the beginning, though, I know that is not always easy because you must learn to get used to incorporating something new into your already busy schedule.

I have heard several people say they fall asleep, and, in my opinion, it's okay if you need sleep. Your body is attempting to relax and heal itself. You may be exhausted and drained. On the other hand, if you are trying to meditate at a particular time when you are more tired, then consider finding another time when you are more awake.

You can try meditation with or without sounds or guided music if that is easier. Some beginning students sit and do breathing techniques instead because they say it helps their focus. Often, new people like guided meditations until they get more comfortable. I would like to add that a few people love to sit in nature and just listen to the sounds around them. By doing so, you are simply being present in your surroundings and noticing the quiet. Now and then, just going out for a walk without any electronic device is enough to calm the mind as well.

During the meditation process, don't worry if you can't see anything or feel like you cannot experience something. The most important aspect is to sit silently to try and calm your thinking mind.

To get the most benefit from meditation, avoid noisy spaces and turn off your phone. You don't want sudden loud sounds pulling you out of the meditative state. Trust me, it's a horrible feeling, leaving you a little disoriented.

If you live in a busy household, I might suggest doing it later in the evening. I know people, especially moms with children that say that it's challenging to find a quiet space in the house. You could do it during your kid's nap time or set your alarm to go off a few minutes earlier in the morning. Do yourself a favor, though, and make sure that you have at least stepped out of bed to wake yourself enough before the meditation if you choose early morning. Otherwise, you may find you fall back asleep. Another idea is that you can go to your car during lunch break to meditate or even to a park. It would help if you found what works best for you.

When preparing to meditate, ensure that you are practicing good breathing. It's helpful to take in deep breaths, holding the breath and then fully exhaling. You might need to do this several times, carefully concentrating on your breathing. You may notice that your body begins to feel lighter and looser or more relaxed. Allow this to happen and then start to let go of the everyday thoughts. If they come into your mind, tell them that you will come back to them. The time to meditate is yours, and you deserve it because what you can achieve through regular meditation of just 10-20 minutes every day will improve your overall well-being.

A couple of tips to share with you on meditation are listed below.

- Find a safe, quiet space where you are not disturbed.
- Practice deep breathing
- Set your intention and focus, and allow yourself enough time to meditate.
- Don't allow yourself to get consumed with the idea that you can't do it.
- Allow yourself to go with the flow.
- Try lighting a candle in a quiet room if it helps to stare at something.
- Recognize that many people need several attempts to calm the mind.
- Try finding a regular time and place if it helps.
- Release expectations on yourself to meditate.
- Know that it's normal for your mind to wander at the beginning.
- Meditation is training the mind to focus and relax.
- Everyone, including children, can meditate so you could find time for the whole family to do it together.

The tips listed here are only a small sampling to help. Find what works best for you.

Chapter 11
What Are Spirit Guides And Can They Help?

You might have heard the term spirit guide or angelic guides that are Divine beings always surrounding, guiding, and protecting us on our journey through life. It's believed that we can have many guides during our lifetime, but one or two that stay with us from birth. It's thought that a spirit guide is only a general term, and you should know that many things can represent them. Guides come in different shapes and sizes that many people theorize: animals, ancestors, archangels, guardian angels, shamans, goddesses, star seeds, and extra-terrestrials. It's believed that some guides have incarnated, while others have not.

When trying to meet your guides, don't worry about who they are. Don't even get consumed with knowing their names. I know many students, including myself, at the beginning that gets led to believe that you must know your guides to do the work in psychic mediumship. It is not valid in my opinion; however, I feel that you must develop a solid faith that they are there for you. Learning to trust that a Higher Power is always surrounding you, ready to assist when you ask, is essential.

Your guides and angels are there for support, and the belief is that that they can only intervene and help when you ask for them too. While I feel this is true, I also am aware that your guides will assist when they think you are in danger of diverting from your life course. This path is something that got designed before you were born. Some call that a life or soul contract that got created to help your soul learn life lessons. It is similar to a road map with the goals your soul sets for itself.

You might already be aware of your guides or have considered that you have angels that have been watching over you. If not, think back on your life and try and remember a time where you felt that an angel must have been watching out to save you from a disaster. Maybe you have experienced moments in life where you just suddenly realized that you knew something or heard someone from inside your head give you a piece of advice that was helpful.

Our guides are subtle, trusted friends, and there for a reason. You need to believe. Remember I mentioned earlier, having the faith of a tiny mustard seed? It's true, and if you can release doubt that you are alone and realize that something bigger exists than you in the universe, then you are truly ready to get started on this journey forward.

Now that I have given you a little understanding of your guides, let's discuss how we can learn to meet them or feel their presence. Before I do, however, I want to state that spirit guides will not make you psychic. They can help with your life, but the ability comes from your Creator and is already present within you. Your guides can help provide you with information and help pass on messages and signs, but their main job is to help you find your way while allowing you to make mistakes to learn what your soul needs.

So, what is their role in your mediumship, you ask? Quite simply to help assist you in finding the tools and knowledge to bring about your goals. Once you have asked for their help, they can often provide the guidance, protection, and control needed. Sometimes, I have frequently felt that my guides helped me set up my readings and deliver the right messages with the proper love and healing. When it comes to my readings with a client, also known as a sitter, I have found them helpful with arranging the communication that works best for me as the medium. They know, in my opinion, exactly how I work and what information I desire and can help ensure that it gets provided from the Spirit.

It might sound comical, but sometimes I have looked at my spirit guides as not only gatekeepers but as bouncers and assistants, like security or staff providing support at an event.

When I first wanted to meet my guide, I tried guided meditations. Over and over, I used different ones without luck and felt disappointed and frustrated, wondering if they even existed or if I somehow was the one soul who didn't receive a spirit guide. I know now that wasn't the truth. I lacked the faith, but when I surrendered to the idea that I would meet my guide in the time I was supposed to, was when they showed up. One thing I can say for a fact, you can't control the Spirit World. You can't control everything, so don't even try to. If you are someone that struggles with that, then I encourage you to say out loud to your guides and the universe that you wish for help to release it. It won't serve you.

How did I meet my guide? Well, for starters, I took a bath. Seriously, the water helps as a conduit for the energy, and I was able to connect. Plus, when I took the warm bath, I was preparing for bed, and therefore my mind was coming down from the busy day I had. With a relaxed mind, I was able to ask in my head for my guide to present him or herself.

While this worked for me and I could get information, I have since found other ways that people have learned to connect with their guides. Some try and ask questions in their minds and then let go of thinking to allow information to flow where they can journal it or sit in a quiet space to feel, see, hear, etc.

Many people find this best to do it in the evening, even after a quick meditation but before bed. Try different methods without expectation but doing so with a calm mind and body. It can help you enter a state where the guide may find it easier to step forward. Still, some people have fantastic luck simply calling out to their guide to ask for them to present themselves in some way or give them a direct sign. I can almost guarantee that one usually works. The hardest part is recognizing and accepting the signs are from them.

I might add some students feel it's best to sit in the power. I will talk more about what sitting in the power is and how it is valuable to developing mediumship in the next chapter. Sitting in the power allows you to feel your energy, increase and expand your awareness, and feel the energy of your guides. Feeling their presence may be all that you will receive, but that should get celebrated.

Some people may hear them, feel, see, or know that their love and guidance surround them. No matter how you perceive your guide, acknowledge their presence, and thank them for their ongoing support. Always feel that you can ask them to help you grow your abilities and assist with your mediumship.

Chapter 12
What Is Sitting In The Power?

Now that you know that meditation is key to calming your mind let's discuss a crucial element, called sitting in the power or sitting with Spirit. Often students hear that they must learn to sit in the power, and they give me a puzzled look. "Why do I need to do that? Isn't that the same as meditation?" The easy answer is no. It's different, and I will tell you why. Sitting in the power takes actual effort because you learn to discipline your mind, body, and awareness. It takes focus and good breathing techniques to sit in a quiet space where you can learn how to sit in your energy to feel, blend and attune to the Spirit World.

   A medium that learns to sit for Spirit can discover how to properly visualize the expansion of their aura outward and upward, filling it with light while focusing on the breath to grow the power necessary to connect and hold a link with Spirit. It is considered fundamental for communication with Spirit by many great mediums. It's said to feel different for everyone and a building block even if done for just 10 to 20 minutes daily. Some people don't do it every day, but they certainly try to make an effort.

Unlike meditation, where your mind can wander, this is a powerful tool meant to help you achieve the necessary knowledge and understanding of the Spirit World through simply sitting in the energy and blending.

In return, it's theorized that the Spirit World is also learning all about you so they can work to achieve good communication. You see how they operate, and they respond to how you work. Usually, this aspect can be achieved halfway through your sitting in the power or even later after you have realized your power and soul self. You must know what your energy feels like before you can understand and differentiate the presence of Spirit. I hope that makes sense because I know for a few people it can be a little confusing. It's nothing to worry about in terms of making a mistake. It's a simple process, but it does take time, patience, effort, and focus. It may not happen overnight, and that is okay.

There are some helpful, guided sitting in the power meditations online that you can find with a simple search. Below I will provide a small example for you to try on your own.

Preparing:
Find a quiet space where you will not be interrupted. Some people like to be in a dark and small room or even a closet. They find it best when it comes to feeling the energy during the process. It's not my thing, but I know people that swear by it. You can try sitting in the power during the daytime or at night in the dark. It's entirely up to you and what you are comfortable doing.

Also, keep in mind that you will want to find a time that you are not sleepy when you are preparing to sit in the power. It's about focus and discipline, and you want to be at your best to achieve the most with Spirit during the period you are undergoing the session.

Example Process:
Begin to set your intention to open and expand your aura and awareness to attune with the Spirit World. You can tell yourself in your mind or out loud. Slowly, take several deep breaths in, holding it a few moments and then exhaling completely. If your

mind should wander, tell it right away that you need to focus. If you need to take in several more breaths to relax, do so. When you feel lighter and ready, begin to try and visualize a ball of white light around your solar plexus near your abdomen. See the white light spinning and getting bigger and brighter and eventually expanding outward and all around you.

Maintaining your breathing, feel the energy, and become aware of the process. Allow yourself to experience it while continuing to expand your energy and power. It may begin to feel like it's moving well above you and into the ether. You are going up until you can see an even brighter source of energy. As you experience your power, sit with it and allow yourself to immerse fully.

When you feel ready, you can extend your aura out even further to blend with the Source's energy. As you blend, feel it surround and embrace you. This is spiritual energy, and in it, you can build your power. Do this for as long as you can and then when you are done, give gratitude and start your descent, bringing your energy slowly back toward you. Visualize your aura coming down from the ether and into your home and back into your body.

Try this regularly, visualizing the process and feeling the energy. If you struggle seeing it, don't worry; place your intent out and sit quietly, telling yourself through the breathing what you wish to achieve. Slowly in your mind, feel the energy changing, shifting, growing, and making you more aware.

Chapter 13
Can You Tell Me How To Connect?

In this chapter, I will focus on how to link with Spirit. For some of you already connecting or who have experienced a connection, you may find it will be easy, while others of you may struggle. If you have been meditating and know how to shift your consciousness to an altered state where you can receive, you are on the right track.

I will try and keep it simple for those who have yet to experience a connection or need a better explanation. When we are awake and alert, we go about our day utilizing our conscious mind. It's our logical, thinking brain. As mediums, we need to learn how to access more than our conscious mind. We must journey toward opening the door to our subconscious, where all our creativity, inspiration, imagination, and intuition lie.

From there, we set our intention to go ever farther upward toward the superconscious. It's often referred to as the soul self and bridge to the Spirit World where we connect. As we link and communicate through the doorways of our consciousness, we bring the information back down and through our conscious mind to receive, interpret and share.

For many people newly learning, this may seem difficult because there are no set guidelines or steps that will work for every individual. Based on my experience and that of others, I have found that we must find ways to link and communicate with Spirit. Most students have had to meditate, sit in the power, and practice, trying different techniques until they found the magic that worked for them.

I realize that you may be reading this and wondering how you can ever be a medium if there isn't a specific set of steps or guidelines to follow. The long and short answer is that you will need to find what works for you through trying different methods to connect. What I am going to provide is ideas that may help you to link. It's a list of tips and tricks that are commonly used.

When I started developing my mediumship, I discovered how to link through trial and error by practicing and setting an intention. In other words, telling my guides and the universe what I wished to do to yield the results. For me, it was necessary, along with meditation and affirmation.

My mind was constantly busy and needed help to relax so that I could shift my awareness inward. By sitting in the power, I learned how to feel my energy and the presence of Spirit. Over time, I began to receive small tidbits for short durations as my power wasn't yet strong enough to sustain a solid link with Spirit. Most information that I brought in was through one clair and not very precise or seemed to conflict with another clair. Example: I would see Spirit in grayscale where the eyes appeared to be dark, like brown. However, I would hear or feel the eye color was blue. Practicing over and over, I discovered the hearing clair at the beginning was delivering the more precise information. In time, as I continued working with Spirit, I eventually just knew which clairs to trust to give me the most accurate evidence. I learned how to understand better how Spirit was communicating and how I recognize, receive, and interpret.

At the start, there was a great deal of symbolism that I couldn't interpret until I continued to practice, grow my power and understanding of Spirit. Patience was not something that I had, and frequently, I got frustrated. Immediately, I began to tell myself affirmations, which eventually seemed to help. Also,

I found that setting myself in the same space with the tools, candles, prayers, and visualizations was the key to unlocking my mediumship. It was my sacred space. As I developed in time, I can tell you that my process became shorter and the ability to shift my awareness became easier. I hope you will find the path to linking with Spirit by providing you the list of tips below.

Tips To Link With Spirit

Set Intention – What do you desire to happen? Be specific. You can write down what you wish to accomplish, say it out loud, or in your mind.

Prayer - Look for a prayer that you can recite, which makes you feel closer to Spirit. You can also choose to create a prayer to say before you connect.

Breath Work - Sit up straight, become aware of your breath. Slowly breathe in and out to calm and relax your mind. Focus on your ribs expanding and chest lifting on inhale, then release and relax your body on exhale. Coordinate breath and movement together until you feel relaxed.

Visualize - Try a visualization to help move your energy upward.
> *Examples:*
> - See yourself getting in a hot air balloon and going up to the Spirit World.
> - Visualize an elevator that can take you upward to those in Spirit.
> - Imagine yourself taking a staircase to Heaven.
> - See yourself expanding and becoming brighter and rising to the Spirit World.
> - Visualize yourself flipping on or turning up a dimmer light switch.

Affirmation - Create an affirmation that helps your subconscious become aware of what you want it to know, understand and appreciate. It may help people that continually struggle with believing they have the power to communicate with Spirit.

Examples:
- I am a Medium that can communicate with those crossed over.
- I can connect with the Spirit World.
- I am love that can receive from Spirit to help heal myself and others.
- I can communicate with Spirit because I am also Spirit.

Action - Create an action to help yourself shift awareness.

Examples:
- Snap your fingers once to tell yourself you are open to Spirit.
- Clap your hands once or rub them together slightly to open.
- Roll your shoulders back or take a step forward or backward.
- Take a deep breath in, close your eyes, and then open them when ready.

Practice- Find a small group of like-minded beginners to practice with.

Mentally remind yourself to keep going. Patience, trust, and perseverance are essential to remember when moving forward. It's like riding a bike, and one day, it will just happen.

When utilizing the above tips, I encourage you to try them all. You may find that one or two of the ideas works best. You can then incorporate them into the process to open to Spirit, or you may develop your method. Whatever makes you feel lighter, happier, vibrationally higher, and brings you closer to the Spirit World will be best for your connection.

EXERCISE: CONNECTING METHODS

Part I. Create a positive intention.
Write down what you hope to achieve. What is your goal?

_____

_____

_____

_____

Part II. Create a prayer.
Do you have a favorite prayer? If not, create one here.

_____

_____

_____

_____

Part III. Create a visualization.

_____

_____

_____

_____

Part IV. Create an affirmation.

_____

_____

_____

_____

Part V. Create an action.

_____

_____

_____

_____

Chapter 14
What Are Some Additional Things To Consider?

Timing of Development
I could say that ten thousand times, and I bet in your excitement, you would still feel eager and hopeful that it will happen overnight. I can say that even if you were a gifted psychic with an ability to learn quickly, that you would still need to take steps to develop yourself.

I recognize that many newcomers tend to be impatient and desire to learn quickly. I know I did at the beginning. It was a process. Some people learning do pick up amazingly fast, but if there aren't stages to development, you will find that you are not receiving all that you could be. I believe that if you don't truly take the time to learn, you may get too much in your head. In which case, you won't be helping yourself. You may get led more by your ego. I have seen many psychics stop self-developing because they started and did just enough to get by.

Symbolism and Impressions

Symbols and impressions can be one of the most complex aspects of development because you must practice and work with your guides to understand the signs, feelings, and images you receive. Spirit uses what you know already, including your emotions, memories, and observations, to try and communicate as closely as possible to what they wish to impart. It's not easy, and sometimes even developed mediums receive something from Spirit that is confusing.

When you need more explanation from Spirit, ask to be shown more or in a different way. I can give a couple of helpful tips here. One is to find someone to sit for you for the reading to practice on that is helpful in determining what your impressions, symbols, sounds, etc., might mean. While you never want someone to make something fit, taking everything you receive, you want them to help you develop possible reasons for relevance to their loved ones.

Another tip is to start a journal of symbols to see how you receive and how Spirit works with you. Often you will receive the same way or along the same lines. For example, when I started, I noticed that Spirit was using my memories of movies and television or music to impart symbolism. An old movie star's name or appearance, for instance, might hold strong meaning.

Blockages

This term is the "B" word when I discuss it in classes. Personally, I wouldn't say I like it because it represents something negative to development. I remember when I started and believed that I was blocked. I searched for hours only to discover I wasn't alone. One of the biggest questions from students is often relating to feeling blocked.

Let me address now that we are never blocked. We are only on a break because we need time to relax, release, and let go. Sometimes we need to sit in the power more, but commonly, we need time for self-care. Maybe we have a lot going on at home, at work, or in our minds. We need to settle what is happening around us first and take a rest so that coming back in; we can rise and move beyond.

Sometimes students are moving so fast in development that they get drained. They forget to take care of themselves. Make sure you find time to do things with your family, friends, and even just by yourself. Time alone to regroup, meditate, and just be.

When students come in and book a mentoring and bring this question, I can't help but look at them and then lovingly smile. They always carry with them the worry and doubt that they have lost their ability. The truth is clear. You will never lose your ability. You only step back from it to reclaim your energy. Once your soul feels ready, it will come back stronger. I hope that makes sense. The best thing that you can do is to keep positive and allow the process to unfold. Never doubt or tell yourself you are blocked. Instead, think of it as a loving and compassionate time of pause and reflection for your soul's highest good.

Feeling Bad About Your Reading

This subject can be super challenging for all mediums, not just new beginning students. Let me say now that not every reading you will have will be perfect. You are human and simply expected to do the best you can. If someone comes to you and makes statements that are hurtful or full of doubt, or if you have trouble making sense of what you receive, let it go. Never hold on to the energy and let it eat at you. Instead, accept that sometimes you will have a sitter that won't be able to comprehend, remember or take what you provide.

You may have great information coming in from a loved one, but the sitter is hyper-focused on what they wish to receive from the session. Your sitter may not remember the memory that Spirit is imparting, or the sitter may not be the only one that Spirit is trying to give a message. It could be another relative that Spirit is trying to contact to provide messages. It does happen. Accept it and smile, telling your sitter that if they feel someone in their family is willing to accept the message, please pass it on.

Also, sometimes, especially at the beginning, we don't always understand the symbols and meanings, and we interpret them wrong. We focus too much and try to analyze it and then perfect it. We may completely get absorbed in our ego as well. Perfectionists will try and do this. I know because that was me at one time. Let go of trying to be constantly correct and accept yourself as only the bridge communicating what you know and receive.

Lastly, if you have a reading that didn't flow smoothly, talk to your guides and those in Spirit to have them lovingly assist you in understanding. They will do their best to work with you when you ask for their help. It's been my experience that they will go out of their way to communicate what you need to know. Whatever you do, don't let it consume you. Let it go, take a walk, meditate, or do something you are passionate about to raise your energy. Release and cut the cords, knowing you did your best.

Cutting Cords and Clearing Your Energy
Cutting and clearing can be done after your reading as easily as saying it aloud in a closing prayer or statement. An example, "At this time, I cut all cords and release them. I now send all the energy back that is not mine and bring in my energy I have shared." Some people use actions, like snaps, claps, or take showers. You can visualize a golden light coming down and clearing away the energy, sending it all down into the earth.

Practicing With Others
Whenever you can, find people to exchange readings. It's best, in my opinion, to work with others who recognize mediumship and what you are going through. I share this piece because if you work with people who are not in complete understanding, they may not be able to help you where you can most benefit.

Find groups that practice either locally or online. You can do them virtually now, where people from all over the world meet in what is called mediumship circles. Many people still meet at Spiritualist churches or local metaphysical stores. Find a tribe that you feel most comfortable and accepted.

If a group doesn't provide a loving and non-judging environment, move on and find one that does. Better yet, start one with a small group of mediums. If you practice regularly, you will find that coming together on an energetic level will help you raise your vibration and power to connect and communicate with Spirit. Each time you practice in a dedicated space with others, you will form a bond and meeting that Spirit won't want to miss on the same day and time. Your loved ones will be excited and ready to share with you as much as you them.

When Your Sitter Can't Take Anything
If you read above what I said regarding having a poor reading, you will know that sometimes it will happen, and you will just have to release it. In mediumship, we sometimes call it getting "no's." It's a part of the work we do, and you are best to ignore it and move on. Never take it to heart or allow your ego to interfere. Every medium gets them, and no one is 100%.

Am I Making It Up
This topic comes up frequently from students at the beginning. They feel that what is coming in couldn't possibly be from Spirit. It comes in so subtly that what is received feels like it's something they imagined. Remember that your clairs can and may feel like that. It's best to continue to sit in the power and practice. When you do that, you learn better focus, differentiation of your energy from Spirit, and most importantly, trust. You will have greater assurance and faith in what you receive because you know how Spirit works with you. Eventually, it should start to feel right when you receive something from Spirit rather than your imagination.

Can All Spirits Come Through
Spirits are like the living. They can get busy and can't always make it to everything even though they want to. Sometimes Spirits that come through will need to communicate a message, especially of healing and closure. They may or may not always be ones that your sitter is willing and wanting to hear from in the Spirit World. If that happens, it's best to share with your sitter that sometimes a Spirit will come through to tell you that over on the other side, they have seen, felt, and discovered how they treated you in life. They wish to give apologies to help you both move forward.

Suppose you have a sitter that is wanting a specific Spirit to come forward. In that case, you should be honest and tell them that you will do the reading and provide the messages from who comes through in Spirit but that you are not capable of ensuring a specific loved one will step forward.

It is possible sometimes to ask for a loved one to come through by setting an intention. It can be done by either the sitter or yourself as the medium simply by loving thought. You can do this easiest by asking out loud or in your mind for the Spirit to come through. If you find that you are unsuccessful, don't get upset. Let your sitter know that their loved one is close by and doing well but couldn't be reached just for that specific time and day. Tell them not to worry.

A little tip I can give you that I do is that sometimes I ask for the name of any loved one that didn't come through toward the end of my reading with the sitter. I have found that this works nicely, and the sitter is appreciative. Also, some Spirits I have found will come through better to some mediums that have developed themselves more and have more power. I have heard other mediums discuss this phenomenon as well. It's just something to consider and not necessarily the whole truth. We are all students learning and have different abilities, strengths, and experiences.

Watch Out For The Ego

We all have an ego, and it's not a bad thing. If you can learn balance, you can use it for good. It's motivating and can help you with confidence in being a medium.

The trouble that I often see is that students finally make links, start doing regular readings, and believe they are all-powerful. Yes, you can help others, but never forget where you came from or think you are better than another. Remember, you are human and work for Spirit. They wish for you to help their loved ones, not hurt them. Be mindful of your attitude and allow yourself to be wrong without letting your ego get bruised.

Sometimes advanced students get ahead of themselves and need to work through the common issue of their ego. We are all in this together and students of Spirit. Each of us should help one another rise rather than trying to come off better than another.

Do yourself a favor, and every so often in your development, check in with inner self. Ask your guides to help you heal your soul to make you a better medium capable of receiving greater healing messages to aid your sitters. You will find that you will become an even more powerful vessel for Spirit, but never let it go to your head. If it does, step back and give gratitude, allowing yourself to realize you are simply the conduit.

Know Your Limits and Boundaries

Boundaries are essential. Too often, we wear ourselves down in all our excitement during development. Once we have made that link, something happens. We get validation, and finally, we conclude we ARE mediums. Just remember that as you develop to step back and breathe. Spend time doing self-care, as I mentioned when I discussed blockages.

Learn to maintain your boundaries as well with others living and in Spirit. It's best at the beginning to know that you are always in control of when Spirit comes to you. Often, people starting will say that they are seeing and feeling Spirit all the time. They don't know how to shut it down. I think the answer to this is to remember that shutting it down is simply dimming the switch and going about your day normally.

Just because you suddenly realized you are a medium doesn't mean that you must go around telling everyone or feeling like a victim. You are in full control. Ask your guides for help with this in your mind or out loud and stick with your intention. If you want Spirit to only communicate during your working hours, then so be it! Ask and then, with patience and diligence on your part, allow it to manifest in time.

I used to have issues with this initially, but I realized I had the power to make the change. Within a short time, it worked. Just make sure you don't make exceptions and break your own rules. What you put out to the universe or show is acceptable will become your reality.

Spirit does not come to you to be a bother, they are simply excited, and if you are always open for business, they will come, sit, and wait for their turn. If you have hours of operation, they will come back because they respect your time too.

When Nothing Happens During A Reading
If you find that you sit down with someone to read them, only to discover that Spirit is nowhere to be found, don't panic. Simply take some deep breaths, and then set your intention for a connection and try again. If you must try some of the different tips, I suggested in an earlier chapter, do it. Whatever you do, don't get anxious and block yourself from receiving. Let your ego know that you are capable of receiving in the event you start to believe that you can't do it.

Consider thinking of a time you connected and had a great reading. Remind yourself of your ability and let go of whatever you feel is standing in your way.

If you have tried without success, nicely let your sitter know that you will need to reschedule for another day. Don't blame yourself or the sitter. Let go and walk away with love and grace. Think about taking time off to get rest and do self-care. Check-in with your guides and spend time sitting in the power. You may simply need to refuel your energy.

Ethics In Mediumship
This topic is one that I believe is especially important. What one person thinks is okay, another might get hurt feelings. It may be the perception in many cases for what is considered right or wrong, but I also believe in using common sense, respect, and intuition.

If it feels wrong, or you question whether you should say or do something, consider just walking away. Don't act out of ego or say something to seem bigger, better, or get attention.

One of the greatest things you can do, in my opinion, is self-heal. Work to release any past hurts, anger, or frustration. When you can see your soul and other souls here learning life lessons, you will start to realize that no one is perfect, and everyone is capable of making mistakes. That's how we grow. Look back on your past with love and forgiveness to yourself and others. By doing this, you will help yourself ethically during your readings. Sometimes how a medium connects, receives, and interprets from Spirit will determine how they have worked through their own personal dilemmas over the years.

Ethically, you are coming from a better place because you won't be holding anger or have any feelings other than love during your readings, no matter who comes through to you for help and healing of their loved one. Why is this important? Because I have personally seen some people struggle with readings due to ego and previous hurts. They could not comprehend or relate the healing messages without filtering it through their unhealed past first.

When you heal, you let go and can suddenly become a vessel that can empathize with Spirit and the sitter. You will have worked through your hurts to recognize and understand what is getting communicated with love from Spirit.

With ethics also comes knowing when to step forward to give messages from Spirit. I bring this up because we often try to share messages with people who may not want them when we realize we are mediums. This behavior is operating more from ego, in my opinion. You must remember everyone has a right to maintain their boundaries, and it's out of respect that you restrain yourself.

Sometimes Spirit will come through to you for a person that may not be ready. Some people are not accepting of mediumship. You should understand or consider that if someone wants a reading, they will come to you. If Spirit comes to me when I am with someone who is not asking for a reading, I quietly, in my mind, tell Spirit that I can't deliver the message in the manner they want. I will, however, gladly try and communicate it in a way that doesn't upset the sitter.

An example might be an older gentleman in Spirit coming forward for his wife. While she tells you about her late husband and how much she misses him, he is next to you, saying how beautiful she looks. As a medium with ethics, consider telling the lady, "I want you to know how lovely you look today. I'm sure your husband is looking down smiling."

If that feels strange to you or you find that you don't know the person, then consider it best to tell Spirit that you don't just deliver messages because of ethics. Tell Spirit that if they truly desire to get a message through, to help you find a way that opens that door ethically. You will be amazed at what Spirit can accomplish when excited and determined to pass on a message.

Lastly, if you feel you receive anything from Spirit that could come across as fearful, unpleasant, or painful, be mindful. You could be misinterpreting what you received and what Spirit actually wants you to relay. If you feel it best to avoid discussing something you are uncertain of, bypass it not to upset your client. If you are sure of something presented from Spirit that seems like a memory of pain but is coming forward to you to help the sitter heal, then use words of compassion and grace. You can ask your guides to help you find the words to say with warmth, tenderness, and empathy. Always remember that when you work with Spirit, you are the medium that is ultimately in charge of ensuring your sitter is leaving with love and healing.

Protection
Often people discuss methods to ensure their protection from the Spirit World. I know many teachers, books, and videos that discuss the need to protect when working with both psychic and mediumship abilities. In my opinion, it is more important to have protection from the living. If you ask me now, the Spirit World is of perfect love and is not full of the fearful energy that the living holds within and around them.

In the past, I used different methods to protect myself while doing work with Spirit. While I no longer feel it is necessary for me, I understand that some people think they still need it. Some believe that dark forces will attempt to harm. To me, that is a statement coming from fear that needs to be addressed and healed in time.

Now, once I learned my strength and trusted in my God power and grew my abilities, I saw only love. What you place out to the universe, you will get back. If you believe that something dark will come to seek harm, you are placing that out into the universe and the most powerful place of all... Your MIND.

Don't allow yourself ever to believe that anything has power over you. I said it earlier in the book. Own your energy and keep your mind focused on the good in everything you do, and that is what you will reap in return.

Now, I understand that some people need time to discover their power, so I encourage you to ask your Creator, your guides, and angels for their help. They will gladly assist you and always provide loving protection and comfort.

Finally, I wish to bring up that for some people, the idea of protection is their intention and action. They need to have a ritual, much like the action to link with Spirit to know and feel security. That is fine, and I agree. Also, you should know that going about your daily life; you are likely picking up other people's energy.

There are people in society, not all living in harmony. Thoughts are getting sent out in the universe daily that may feel heavy or unpleasant, especially if they get directed to you. It is my advice to use protection, especially if you are sensitive to the energy around you.

There are many ways that people can call in protection to their energy. You may already have a way that works for you, and that is great. If you don't, then consider the following ideas.

- Visualize a golden ball of white light, and you are sitting inside it. Nothing can penetrate this bubble around you. It shields you from thoughts and the energy of others.
- Say a prayer of loving intention or your favorite known prayer.
- Place a set of mirrors around your energy that faces outward so that energy can bounce off.
- Ask your guides and loved ones for their protection.
- Use crystals or create a sacred space where you connect and clear the energy from each reading.
- Create a type of action and a saying that gives you a feeling of power over your energy field.

Grounding

What is grounding? If you have already started down your path, you may have already heard of it. Some of you may wonder what it is. Grounding can help you feel calmer, relaxed, and centered as you work on your abilities. The benefits of grounding yourself include emotional and mental clarity. You may find that it will help with your everyday life and not just when you are doing readings.

If you are newly awakening, you could have an excess of emotion and overwhelm. Some of that may or may not be your energy. As you go about your day, you want to be at peace and focused on increased awareness. You will find that meditating will be a huge stress reliever, which will improve your overall health in the end.

It would be beneficial if you tried to do your best to keep your body, mind, and soul at the most peaceful, relaxed state it can be to receive from the Divine. By grounding yourself, you are allowing that excess energy to have someplace to go. Grounding can be done in several ways because there is no right or wrong way if your intention exists.

Some people choose to visualize it, while others prefer to say it or go outside and walk in nature. You can go barefoot in the grass, garden, walk along the seashore, or sit quietly in your yard, breathing in the fresh air.

If you are a visual person, you may want to try closing your eyes and seeing yourself standing on grass barefoot while cords come out of the bottoms of your feet and enter the earth's surface. Allow those cords to travel down for as far as you can see. Another visualization is imagining yourself as a large tree with roots extending down into Mother Earth.

If you would prefer to speak your intention, then put your intent out by stating an affirmation. Some people say the same statement each time, and some say a few quick words. Please do what you are comfortable with, as it is my experience that the universe will always comply.

What Teachers, Classes, And Mentors Are Best
Look around for teachers, classes, and mentors that have reviews that look real and reputable. Do the research and go with your gut on what is best for you. In my opinion, we learn something from everyone. Good or bad, you will discover what you need to know. It's a journey, and sometimes one door leads to another and another. Trust it.

Positive Mindset

I can't tell you how important it is to be positive. You are human, and no doubt, you will have days that you are tired, cranky, frustrated, or even mad. It's okay to get upset but learn to adopt a positive mindset as you go about your days. You will be surprised how saying something loving to yourself or others will make you feel. It will help to raise your vibration, and having a higher vibration is so vital, in my opinion, when working with Spirit.

You are helping your body, mind, and soul to radiate peace and joy. When you are happy, you are more relaxed, inspired, and brighter. You want to be lighter and calmer, so work on smiling and putting out happy thoughts.

At first, it may be challenging, but over time, it should get more comfortable. In my own life, I know that I had days where I was in a low place, and when I would practice putting out happy thoughts to the universe, it felt fake. I thought I was trying to deceive myself. However, over time, I noticed that it got easier as I went about my day with loving affirmations and reminders. Soon, I felt lighter, and I didn't have to convince myself. I'm not saying that I don't still have those days, but once I learned, I trusted and knew that it would pass, and brighter days would return.

Love Yourself

You need to love and look at yourself as a healthy and beautiful soul. You have been brought down into a physical body to experience, learn, and grow. Above all things, to learn about love. That includes loving others, the universe, the earth, and all the elements and animals on the planet. Most importantly, is that you need to learn to love yourself and release judgments. You are wonderful, unique, and perfect in every way.

If you feel anything but love, then you are living with fear. Don't be consumed by your shadow self or ego. Remember I said the ego could help motivate us? Let it assist you positively, rather than slow you down.

You need to understand that you are human and having a human experience. You won't always be correct or do the right things. You will make mistakes, which is okay, but you need to release the idea that you must be perfect.

Remind yourself that you are always doing excellent work, and no matter your progress, you are going upward. It may take you a while, but the more you release the judgments and learn to love yourself for who you are, the better and farther you will go.

Chapter 15
Final Words

In closing this book, I would like to say a few final words to help you grow your abilities and soul. Every action, thought, and intention of love that you put into your development will eventually lead you to your goal of becoming a psychic medium or spiritual medium. The difference is only what you decide to call yourself and with what you are comfortable saying.

As you go about finding the techniques that will help you link and communicate, keep yourself grounded and in a place of peace. You want to remember patience, trust, and faith. I wish to restate from what I said earlier in the book that nothing happens overnight. You can't take a class on the weekend, watch a webinar, attend a retreat or even read this book and instantly hold successful and strong links for good communication with Spirit. There is work involved.

Time, dedication, and effort will help you move forward on your journey. However, I hope that this book has provided you with basic, simple ideas and given you some essential knowledge to at least get started. I will say to you now that there is a wealth of knowledge in books, classes, and videos to discover when you are ready. As you go through the learning process, find out what feels best for your journey. You have the power and hold the key to your future growth and success. Go for it and believe in yourself!

Printed in Great Britain
by Amazon